Sir Bobby Charlton:

The People's Champion Who United Millions: The Untold Story of the Red Devil Who Never Faded

Daxton Thomas

Copyright page

Table of contents

Introduction

English professional footballer Sir Robert Charlton CBE (11 October 1937 – 21 October 2023) was a left winger, offensive midfielder, and center midfielder. He was a member of the England squad that won the FIFA World Cup in 1966, the same year he won the Ballon d'Or, and is regarded as one of the best players of all time.

In 1967 and 1968, he came in second place in the Ballon d'Or vote. He spent almost all of his club football career playing for Manchester United, where he gained a reputation for his aggressive propensities, midfield passing skills, fierce long-range shot, fitness, and stamina.

On October 21, 2023, Sir Bobby Charlton, the king of English football, died. He was 85 years old. His passing rocked the football community and left an emptiness that can never be filled.

Greatness, both on and off the field, is left behind by Charlton. He was a genuine football legend, and the annals of football history will always remember his name.

Charlton was a crucial contributor to England's victory in the 1966 FIFA World Cup as a member of the team. He was also a successful goal scorer for England, tallying 49 goals in 106 games.

In addition to winning the World Cup, Charlton also captured the Ballon d'Or that year. His accomplishments are unrivaled, and he is regarded as one of the best players of all time.

At Manchester United, where he spent his whole club career, Charlton won three First Division championships, one FA Cup, and the European Cup. He has scored 249 goals in 758 appearances for the club, making him its all-time greatest scorer.

A true gentleman of the game, Charlton. He was a role model for aspiring football players all across the world because he was consistently kind and modest.

Although his passing is a tragedy for the football community, his legacy will endure. He was a genuine legend, and we will always remember his name.

The loss of Sir Bobby Charlton will last a lifetime.

Chapter one

Childhood Dreams: The Making of a Football Prodigy

One of the greatest midfielders of his generation was Bobby Charlton, whose full name is Sir Robert Charlton. He played football for England in the past. He was born in Ashington, Northumberland, England, on October 11, 1937.

The north-east is where English football's roots are the deepest, and his tale appeared to reach there as well. In Northumberland's Ashington, his father worked as a coal miner. On Fridays, when his father picked up his pay, the young Bobby would occasionally go with him to the pit head.

The youngster observed men emerging from the mine shafts, covered in coal dust, and beaming with relief. The men who were waiting to take their turn at the front looked dejected. That would not be his fate, nor would Jack, his older brother, who would share his finest day, be Jack's. After all, the legendary Jackie Milburn of Newcastle United and England was their mother's second cousin. Cissie Charlton had four brothers who were all working professionals. In the blood it was.

Bobby preferred football to bird watching, fishing, and all of his other boyhood hobbies in the rural area surrounding a mining town. The football squad at his school wore red shirts with laces around the neck and shorts made out of blackout curtains.

Early marking led to him signing up with United's ground staff at the age of 15. As he saw Charlton make room in the starting lineup for another divinely appointed talent, Duncan Edwards, one can only imagine Matt Busby clutching himself to be sure he wasn't dreaming.

Munich altered him. Some claim that after surviving the crash that killed eight of his comrades, including Edwards, he never truly smiled again. He developed a reputation for being rigid; there were tense interactions with Jack, who was much more laid-back and open, and with George Best, whose destructive hedonism he regarded with suspicion, although in 2007, he had no qualms about starting the Irishman up front alongside Denis Law in his own all-time United XI.

Later, it was said that he was among the United directors who opposed hiring José Mourinho to succeed Alex Ferguson in 2013 because they disapproved of the Portuguese coach's confrontational tactics.

People thought he was gloomy and still think so about him, Pat Crerand wrote in his memoirs. He might be, but Bobby is not who the general public sees him to be. Although he is not a social person, he is a decent man. Only some people make Bobby feel at ease. He was a completely different person when you saw him with his friends, Shay Brennan and Nobby Stiles. He was witty and upbeat.

Charlton would define his affiliation with football as an addiction rather than a profession.

When he received the ball during the pre-match warm-up, Crerard, who played with him when they were both grown men, also had insight into that: He was like a kid with a new toy. Although he was an excellent player, he was never able to get past the rush of having the ball at his feet.

All the finest performers give off this impression, creating an unconscious connection between their inner child and the viewers. Because of it, Charlton was able to join Puskas and Di Stéfano, Pelé and Eusébio, and Best and Cruyff at the highest table of his time.

The great tragedy he had experienced at the age of 20 as well as the price of his survival and our awareness of that deeper impact undoubtedly contributed to his presence in the match that emanated a seriousness of purpose and a sense of distance—never aloof, but somehow apart.

He had a genuine life before, and that is where he continued to live. His father was working 800 feet below the earth at the coal face the day he scored both of England's goals in their victory over Portugal to go to the 1966 championship, having concluded that asking for another day off might be pushing it.

It came out that his emotions were barely visible beneath that modest, austere exterior. He shed tears twice during his 1969 appearance on This Is Your Life: once when the story reached the disaster, and once earlier when Milburn addressed him—and the television audience—from the Ashington recreation ground where he had gone on Sundays to watch and encourage the young relative.

Bobby Charlton rose to prominence from that soggy field. Two steam engines pushed the vintage Direct-Orient Express on one night in June 1968 as it made its way to Istanbul from Bulgaria to Yugoslavia. Two stern-looking guards entered the third-class cabin, rousing the napping passengers and demanding to see the documents. A young couple was approached and given two passports with dark blue covers. After glancing over their passports, they turned to face one another.

One person exclaimed, Eeeng-lish! One yelled, Boh-by Charrrl-ton! at the other. The two were grinning. I'll stop here.

There was only one Bobby Charlton, a survivor, pioneer, role model, record-breaker, and high achiever who won the World Cup. The best football tale ever told was his.

Chapter two

Glory Days at Old Trafford: Triumphs with Manchester United

Manchester United initially enticed 10-year-old Bobby Charlton during the 1948 FA Cup final. He had been invited to a teammate's home to see United play Blackpool in what turned out to be a classic final after playing for East Northumberland Boys in the morning. He subsequently recalled: It was from that day that I wanted to be a footballer and join Manchester United, even though he and his friends missed a large portion of their 4-2 victory due to playing football outside.

Sixty years later, on a rainy night in Moscow, when United had defeated Chelsea in the Champions League final, Charlton led the players up to get their medals while also receiving one himself. His jacket was soaked through. He had served as a football figure on the club's board since 1984, when Sir Matt Busby retired, and he remained very prominent until the onset of dementia forced his retirement from public life.

In the winter of late 1989 and early 1990, when a costly team struggled, Alex Ferguson's support was maintained in large part because of Charlton's faith in the ability of the man who had broken the Scottish Old Firm with Aberdeen. A brief exchange between Ferguson and Charlton at the 1986 World Cup in Mexico served as the seed for what would grow into a deep friendship. That faith would be repaid many times over.

Both would refute Ron Atkinson's accusation that Charlton had taped up the then-Scotland manager, even though Ferguson acknowledged Charlton had remarked that if I ever decided to move to England, I should let him know. Atkinson was fired by United the following November.

Charlton was a familiar face in the directors' box, and to fans under the age of 50, he represented the status quo. Although it was his longest-serving position, he had many different roles at Manchester United. He joined the Busby Babes, the greatest uprising of young football talent English sport had ever seen, on New Year's Day 1953.

The young Charlton, with his fair hair and beard, plunged himself into the theaters, cafes, and dances of Mancunian life, far from his colliery village of Ashington.

Busby, known as The Old Man, had spies all over the place, but his vigilance allowed young players to have fun within limits. The time Charlton spent hanging around with friends like Eddie Colman, who exuded Salfordian swagger both on and off the field; David Pegg, a handsome Yorkshireman who was popular with female supporters; and Duncan Edwards was characterized by Charlton as paradise in his autobiography.

The most talented of Busby's golden harvest was Charlton, whose mother, Cissie, had entertained a group of scouts in Ashington: They even drank from the same brew of tea without realizing it. When John Giles, one of the best players of the 1960s and 1970s, first saw the talent of Charlton, a few years older, in training, he admittedly thought about returning to Ireland right away.

Then, eight comrades perished in the tragedy in Munich. Two Busby assistants who provided fatherly advice, Tom Curry and Bert Whalley, also passed away. Charlton's paradise was lost without them. After recovering from minor injuries in Ashington, he traveled to Manchester, where his demeanor began to shift almost immediately.

A young Bobby would frequently sing to himself in the house, according to his brother Jack, but after Munich, our kid stopped singing.

15 days after the collision, Cissie informed him of Edwards' passing while she was at Ashington. That was the toughest to take.

The years following Munich, of which no mention was tolerated at the Cliff training ground, were a sincere struggle for United, who flirted with relegation and rebellion against a reduced, grieving Busby. Without his friends nearby, a 20-year-old with survivor's guilt had enormous responsibility thrust upon him.

Up until Busby was able to assemble a second great United squad when the pressure could once again be distributed, Charlton frequently struggled with his form. He had established himself as one of the best players in the world of football by the mid-1960s after switching from the wing, where he spent the majority of the post-Munich years, and was perhaps the best player in England.

He danced through a time of heavy pitches and crunching tackles as a midfield general of remarkable grace with a cannonball blast off either foot. He was successful as well. There were jitters as United came within one win of winning the 1966–1967 First Division, but teammate Brian Kidd claims that Charlton calmed everyone down by telling them to give me the ball and we'll be fine.

The United Trinity statue on the forecourt of Old Trafford features Charlton alongside Denis Law and George Best, but the three men could not have been more dissimilar. Charlton passed away at the age of 86. Law, known as Denis the King and beloved by the Stretford End, was a prolific goal scorer who played the game with a likable blend of a beaming smile and a volatile temper that frequently erupted. Best, who was extraordinarily talented and gorgeous to look at, would go on to represent living fast and pushing talent to the limit, but when he was in full flow, he was seductive and fully deserved the title of Britain's first football hero.

As a playboy receiving sacks of female fan mail every morning and a family man who was married at age 22, Charlton and Best made for an awkward alliance. Both passionately disagreed with the other's lifestyle, and despite being cordial in public regarding their teammate's football skills, there were also times of friction regarding events that occurred on the field. But when Best's drunkenness finally caught up to him and he was dying in the

Cromwell hospital in November 2005, Charlton flew to London to be by his side.

Charlton did not pay Best the trite platitudes that one might anticipate from someone with whom he had never shared a close relationship in the hours following his passing. Instead, Charlton opted for introspection to process the loss of a player who, in his words, was on a par, if not better than anyone you can name. Then he began to reflect on his contribution to the outcome. Who knows if we had leaned a little toward George and tried to help him instead of being hostile to him, which I was?

What Charlton and Best had in common was a natural shyness that was probably incompatible with being a great football player. Whereas Best desired obscurity, Charlton's clipped, austere public presence caused many to write him off as being chilly. It was an unfair assessment because he could never have had older brother Jack's all-American charm that captured the hearts of the Irish people.

As years passed by and anniversaries occurred, there were numerous teary-eyed memorials to friends who had died in Munich. Tears were shed after the 1966 World Cup final victory and were shared with Busby on the Wembley field following the 1968 European Cup victory. Charlton did not even approach the table during the celebration dinner that followed the latter victory. He had been unable to get out of his hotel bed due to mental fatigue, according to his wife, Norma: He's remembering the lads who can't be here tonight.

Bobby Charlton couldn't help but get all warm and tingly inside when it came to football, especially Manchester United.

Chapter three

The World Cup Triumph: 1966 and Beyond

Gianni Infantino, the president of Fifa, praised Charlton as a football legend whose impact on the game spanned generations, while Geoff Hurst, another member of Charlton's 1966 England team, named him one of the true greats.

Gary Lineker agreed, stating that Charlton was the finest player to represent England. He may not be with us anymore, but he will live on in football history.

Footballers from the past may appear to be playing at half speed in old, grainy video games. Unlike Charlton. Even after 50 years, he still resembles a current football player in every way:

two-footed, bright, and savvy; he possesses the strength of a workhorse and the talent of a maestro.

Even in black and white, the innumerable photos of him firing a cannonball shot past a beaten goalkeeper while the cameraman tries to keep up still make people gasp.

And Charlton's numbers would be remarkable in any period. During his 17 years as a player for Manchester United, he played 758 games and scored 249 goals while winning the FA Cup, three league championships, and the European Cup. He amassed 106 caps for England and set a record with 49 goals, which Wayne Rooney eventually surpassed in 2015.

He was a standout performer at the 1966 World Cup, scoring two goals against Portugal in the semi-final. When Charlton received the OBE three years later, the Observer carried it on the main page with the straightforward yet impactful headline, Cheers for Bobby Charlton. Later, Johan Cruyff selected him as the lone English player for his ideal all-time XI.

Charlton was the ideal English person in more ways than one, though, not just as a footballer. He did as a man as well. He was a living example of Rudyard Kipling's poem If—handling success and failure in the same manner, and he remained modest even though his talents were remarkable.

Since Charlton had survived the Munich air disaster on February 6, 1958, which claimed the lives of 23 people, including eight players and three staff members from the club, United's European Cup victory, in which they defeated Benfica 4-1 at Wembley, was especially poignant.

The impact of that catastrophe was unbelievably profound; according to his brother Jack, Sir Bobby stopped smiling and left his sparkle in the plane's debris.

Bobby participated in all six of our World Cup games during the 1966 Finals, scoring three goals—once in our 2-0 group-stage triumph over Mexico and twice in our 2-1 semifinal victory over Portugal. The only occasion Charlton received a booking while representing England was in the quarterfinal game against Argentina. At the 1970 World Cup Finals in Mexico,

Charlton made four appearances—three of which were as a substitute.

The player later announced his retirement from international football after making his final appearance for his nation in the 3-2 loss to West Germany in the competition's round of eight. With 106 appearances at the time, he held the record for most England international caps ever, although six players have since surpassed him.

While managing Preston North End for the 1973–74 season, Charlton, who had been at Manchester United since 1956, hired his England 1966 teammate Nobby Stiles as player-coach. After the Deepdale club was demoted in 1974, Charlton started juggling playing and managing. He played against

Gillingham twice, both times in the 1974–75 season.

The first was our fifth straight loss, a 1-0 loss at Lancashire on October 22. John Bird, who was unmarked on the edge of the box by a Bobby Charlton corner, scored the game's lone goal. According to Dave Parr's match report, Bird gave goalkeeper Ron Hillyard no chance with a ferocious effort.

Just over a week later, on Wednesday, November 6, the rematch took place. Parr began his match report by writing, The magic of Bobby Charlton was just a dim memory at Priestfield last night as Gillingham produced their best home performance of the season to lift themselves off the bottom of the Third Division. 10,494 spectators showed up to see Charlton, undoubtedly the largest crowd of the season, but Charlton had no impact as Gillingham won as a result of two goals from loaned striker Peter Feely.

The supporters who had gathered to honor Bobby Charlton departed Gillingham, talking not about the great man but rather about the new competitive spirit that might still help Gillingham become a Third Division team.

Charlton managed and played for Preston and Waterford United in Ireland after leaving United in May 1973. He was appointed a director by Manchester United in 1984, and the club declared in February 2016 that they would rename its South Stand in his honor.

After receiving a knighthood in 1994, Charlton and his wife, Lady Norma, went on to become a well-known sight at Old Trafford up until his dementia diagnosis in 2020.

Chapter four

Leadership and Legacy: Sir Bobby Charlton's Enduring Impact

Despite the spread of despair, Charlton is a living illustration of faith in the light of hope that will never go out.

The sparkling success of Charlton did not happen quickly. He has gone through pain, just like every other person. Despite the spread of despair, Charlton is a living example of confidence in a lamp of hope that will never go out. Charlton emerged from the ruins of despair after the devastating Munich air accident on February 6, 1958, which resulted in the deaths of eight Manchester United players, and he helped the team grow into what it is today.

Johnny Berry and Jackie Blanchflower, two survivors from Charlton, were teammates who never played again. Nevertheless, Charlton appeared unaffected by the ordeal and carried on with his football career. Along with manager Matt Busby, who also survived the tragedy, Charlton emerged as a vital figure in the Red Devils' reconstruction.

However, a defining step in his journey to becoming a football icon was when he, at the age of 20, miraculously survived the Munich Air Disaster.

It is difficult to continue a profession after suffering a terrible accident, yet Charlton managed to do so. The most incredible feat Charlton accomplished was guiding MU to three titles in a single season in 1968. MU not only won the European Cup but the FA Cup and English Premier League as well.

For Manchester United and Charlton, who were attempting to reverse their decline, winning the 1969 European Cup was extremely significant. All of the players celebrated after the game. The three members of the MU team who survived the plane crash—Busby, Charlton, and Bill Folks—became the center of attention in the stadium at that point.

Due to the Munich catastrophe, Charlton feels vulnerable on the inside yet fierce on the playing field. Former MU director Martin Edwards observed Bobby crying after beating Benfica in the European Cup final.

Bobby had a lot of emotion that evening. He never hosted a meal. After the game, he was filled with emotion. He fell asleep because he was exhausted. Other players celebrated, but he was overcome with emotion, stated Edwards.

Charlton scored 249 goals while appearing in 758 games for MU overall. Ryan Giggs and Wayne Rooney eventually smashed two marks that stood for years. The perseverance and passion of Charlton still serve as an example for MU.

Even after retiring from playing, Charlton continued to have a big impact on MU's development into the powerhouse it is today. He served as the director of MU for 39 years, during which time he was crucial in luring Sir Alex Ferguson to the team. Ferguson, who was having trouble getting MU to perform well at the outset of his term, was set to be fired, and Charlton vehemently opposed this idea.

This is possible as a result of Charlton's high regard for Ferguson, whom he regarded and respected as Busby's successor. Due to his services, Manchester United honored Charlton in 2008 by erecting a statue of him beside Denis Law and George Best, two other club heroes.

Sir Bobby Charlton was a dynamic player who was successful in several positions, including offensive midfielder, central midfielder, and left winger. Because of the intimate connection between his brilliant career and Manchester

United, he came to represent the club's enduring spirit.

The influence of Charlton on football goes far beyond the field of play.

Football fans all across the world still love the World Cup victory, and one of the greatest England goals in history is Charlton's strong long-range strike against Portugal in the 1966 World Cup semifinal.

The impact of Sir Bobby Charlton goes far beyond the football field. Incredibly, he is the only Englishman to have won the Ballon d'Or, the European Cup, and the World Cup. He had a long-lasting impact on the sport; therefore, his influence went beyond only his playing career.

Beyond football, Charlton wrote his autobiography titled My Manchester United Years in 2007 which offered insights into his illustrious career and the development of football at the time.

While many people honor Sir Bobby Charlton for his well-known career accomplishments, these lesser-known details give a more nuanced picture of a guy who is a genuinely complex great of the game.

Chapter five

From Hampden to Wembley: Sir Bobby Charlton's Six Sublime Symphonies

The 86-year-old legend for Manchester United and England changed games with his incredible skill and goals.

Scotland defeated England 4 to 0 on April 19, 1958, at Hampden Park, Glasgow.

Charlton, who was chosen on the left wing, believed he had been called up for England too soon. The 20-year-old stated, I believe they felt terrible for me because of Munich.

Even though England sent the young United star to the first of his four World Cups in 1958,

Charlton did make his international debut by scoring in front of 134,000 spectators at Hampden to honor the occasion. A Scottish audience had the pleasure of witnessing the first of many goals he would score for England, sprinting onto a pass from Tom Finney and firing a potent shot on the run.

The sound of the ball slamming against the net is still fresh in my mind, said Charlton. After that, there was nothing but stillness.

Borussia Dortmund defeated Manchester United 6-1 on November 11 at the Westfalenstadion in Dortmund.

In 1964–1955, United defeated Leeds for the championship only on goal differential, but several of their victories were convincing, with Charlton, Law, and Best becoming established starters. At Ewood Park, they defeated Blackburn Rovers 5-0, Aston Villa 7-0, and Liverpool 3-0. When Charlton scored a hat-trick against Blackburn, Nobby Stiles, who was watching, said, Bobby played them on his own.

So it was in Europe when United ran into West German Cup champions Dortmund on their way to the Inter-Cities Fairs Cup semifinals, which would later become the Uefa Cup. Inspired by a hat-trick from Charlton, United ended the match in the first leg in West Germany, and Charlton added two more goals at Old Trafford to advance 10-1 overall.

Now that he was playing a more prominent role, Charlton was scoring goals with his potent long-range shooting.

Wembley, London, July 16, 1966: England 2, Mexico 0.

The first goal versus Mexico was perhaps one of the most memorable. Charlton was frequently referred to as one of the greatest goal scorers, if not the greatest.

It was Britain's first goal of the championship they were hosting, and after a somber, scoreless struggle in the opening match against Uruguay and some cynical anti-football on display in the other groups, people started to think the World Cup 66 may be a miserable failure.

By taking up the ball in his half and carrying it until a shot became possible, Charlton was credited with instantly changing that perception and inspiring confidence in both team and country. I picked up the ball quite deep, and I had no intention of shooting at first, he added. I really didn't think they'd let me keep going, but when they did, I just banged it, and it came off so sweetly, she said.

Portugal 1, England 2: Wembley, London, July 26, 1966

Even though England won the tournament, it may seem strange to prioritize the semi-final over the actual final. However, Charlton contributed to the team's success in the 4-2 victory over West Germany by focusing on shadowing Franz Beckenbauer.

Against Portugal in the semifinal, he had a lot more leeway to express himself, and it paid off with the two goals that advanced England to the final.

Except for the possibility that Roger Hunt should have been declared offside, the first goal was somewhat uneventful. However, Charlton's second goal was classic Charlton, as he raced on to Geoff Hurst's square pass and sent a powerful drive past Pereira without pausing. Rather marvelously, photos of the goal show Charlton standing up straight even as the ball enters the goal.

Bobby Charlton had much of his best game of the World Cup, perhaps his best for England, Brian Glanville gushed. His running made gaps, his passing was crisp, and he scored both goals.

Manchester United 3 Real Madrid 3: Bernabéu, Madrid, 15 May 1968

If United had not survived a grueling semifinal against Real Madrid that year, there would have been no Wembley victory over Benfica, and when the home team took a 4-2 aggregate lead in the second leg at the Bernabéu, it appeared as though the Busby-Charlton dream was dead for another year.

At Old Trafford, George Best's lone goal gave United a chance, but Real Madrid promptly erased that advantage with three goals of their own, leaving the visitors with just one goal at halftime. The chances of United making any advancement while Denis Law was injured did not appear promising, but they put up a fantastic fight in the second half and tied the game on goals from defenders David Sadler and Bill Foulkes.

Although Charlton had not made much of an impact, his sobbing on the field at the final whistle revealed how he felt about the accomplishment of making it to the final. Later, he declared that the Bernabéu match was the best one he had ever participated in, surpassing even the World Cup final from two years prior. He said, Real, they were killing us. But after the break, we continued to fight, and they lost.

Wembley, London, May 29, 1968: Benfica 1, Manchester United 4

After winning the World Cup in 1966, Charlton declared there was nothing else for a professional footballer to strive for, yet his best moment at club level was yet to come.

In the end, United defeated Benfica relatively easily, in part because of Alex Stepney's crucial stops for Eusebio, but it's vital to keep in mind that the Lisbon team at the time had almost twice as much European experience as their rivals. Benfica had already won the European Cup, so United was trying to become the first English team to do it.

When the European dream came to fruition that night, Charlton served as captain. The Munich calamity of ten years earlier was brought into sharp relief, and there were moving moments when he handed the trophy to Matt Busby.

After Benfica forced extra time with nine minutes left and Charlton scored the game's opening goal with a rare header from David Sadler's cross, the game was effectively over thanks to goals from George Best and Brian Kidd before the captain added a second-to-round off an incredible victory.

Chapter six

Bobby and Jack Charlton: United in Triumph,

Divided in Life

After the 1966 World Cup final, Jack and Bobby Charlton traveled back to Ashington, their birthplace in Northumberland, where they were welcomed as royalty in a colliery town renamed Charltonville for the occasion.

The Ashington Mineworkers Federation hosted a gala dance that the brothers attended to cap off their night of celebration as they rolled through town in an open-topped Rolls Royce. In August 1966, the Charltons appeared to be returning actors while seated in the vintage Rolls. Never again would they appear to be so close.

Bobby, Gordon, Tommy, and Jack were the family's other three brothers. Due to the family's limited resources, all four children slept in the same bed. While his mother, Cissie, played football with her kids and subsequently served as the local school's head coach, his father, Bob, showed little interest in the sport.

When a plane crashed in the snow in Munich in February 1958, a local shopkeeper had to rush through these streets to inform the boys' mother, Cissie Charlton. The 23 fatalities of the Munich aviation catastrophe, according to many people who knew Bobby, left him with survivor's remorse and lingering emotional suffering.

The Charlton lads, who were paraded throughout Ashington, were never friends when they were little. Jack, who preferred the outdoors, hated having to look out for his younger, more domesticated sibling. They were split apart by family strife in their post-playing lives, but they came together over a horrific event in their latter years. Both passed away from dementia and suffered from pain and memory loss in their final months.

Jack Charlton passed away on July 11, 2020, at the age of 85, from dementia and cancer. Bobby, who was 83 at the time, received the same cruel medical diagnosis four months later. The most well-known and admired English football player vanished from view and has now joined the long list of 1966 World Cup champions who have succumbed to dementia. During Alf Ramsey's later years in suburban Ipswich, Ray Wilson, Nobby Stiles, Martin Peters, Roger Hunt, and both Charlton brothers all suffered from the same illness.

In ways that are as dissimilar as their characteristics, the convergent medical histories of the Charlton brothers serve as a somber contrast to the happy memories each brother left behind.

Bobby would go on to become the understated statesman of English football and a calming influence at Manchester United, where he served as director the entire time Sir Alex Ferguson was in charge. Jack entered folklore in exile as the manager of the Republic of Ireland, taking them to the 1988 European Championship finals and the 1990 World Cup, where they reached the last eight. Jack was angry at not being given an interview when Don Revie quit the England manager's position in 1977.

The two lads who had learned the sport from Cissie on the unruly Ashington fields had different physical characteristics, playing preferences, and personalities. Jack was a strong, aggressive, and towering enforcer. Bobby was a talented offensive midfielder with a knack for accurate long-range shooting. He was shorter, lighter, and more flowy. Tom Finney was the English footballer with the greatest natural potential. On the other hand, Jack once remarked to himself, Playing is the one thing I couldn't do. However, I was skilled at keeping others from playing.

The older man's portrayal as Bobby Charlton's brother did a disservice to his playing career at

Leeds United, where he spent 23 years and made a joint-record 773 appearances before retiring in 1973. Jack was the craftsman, and Bobby was the artist.

Bobby, however, radiated elegance. His talent put him in the middle of a late 1960s global golden generation that included Johan Cruyff, George Best, Pelé, and Eusébio. Bobby's 106 England appearances outnumbered Jack's 35. The two walked out at Wembley on July 30, 1966, to face West Germany, regardless of their differences in talent and character.

The Northumbrian odd pair made up 20% of the outfield unit on England's lone World Cup-winning team due to a genetic oddity. It was a big claim for Ashington's working-class neighborhood, where Jackie Milburn, Cissie's cousin, had been hailed as a hero before the Charltons arrived.

The claim in east London has long been that Bobby Moore, Geoff Hurst, and Martin Peters were all products of West Ham and made up 3/11ths of the England starting lineup. Nearby to the former Upton Park and West Ham's new home at the London Stadium are statues honoring these cockney bragging rights. Ramsey was a native of the nearby town of Dagenham. However, the narrative of the Charlton boys was an even more amazing component of England's 4-2 victory in extra time.

Bobby received a lesson from Walter Winterbottom and later Ramsey at the England level that would ultimately cement his journey to stardom. The underlying message was that he would not be recognized as a great team player if he played his own expressive game in the hard environment of the 1960s. Ramsey instilled in Charlton the idea that he could only fully contribute to England's style of play if he supported the defense and displayed system respect.

Ramsey had a pragmatic approach and was aware of how Brazil had changed the world of football. With the steadfast organizer being the former Ipswich manager, England would rely on what they already knew.

At the center of the mission was Bobby Charlton. At a time when keeping players out of the pub was practically a tactical talent, the England manager went looking for someone receptive, obedient, and sincerely committed.

Bobby had a weak tendency to question The General's authority, as Ramsey's Tottenham Hotspur teammates had nicknamed him.

Jack was a different story. He came off as arrogant and disobedient to Ramsey. The most scathing criticism the England manager could give Jack was to tell him that international teams weren't always made up of the greatest players. Jack was reminded that he was on the team for reasons other than natural talent.

Bobby found the fabricated officer-class brusqueness of Ramsey intimidating. The England team was staying in Hendon, an hour's drive away, and the players encouraged Bobby to address the manager over his selection of Roehampton as the World Cup training facility. Bobby left the meeting feeling dejected. He replied after Ramsey had dismissed him with his usual harshness, Boys, don't ever let me do that again.

And yet, in the 1966 championship game, Jack may have had more of an impact than his younger sibling, who had dazzled in a dazzling 2-1 semifinal victory over Portugal. Bobby had scored both goals with heavy significance, and Jack had given up the penalty in the 82nd minute, which forced England to cling to their lead for the final eight minutes.

The star of that show was Bobby Charlton, not Eusébio, but there would soon be a surprise. Ramsey forced him to man-mark the teenage Franz Beckenbauer for the championship game. The greatest players on either side were mutually nullified by their managers, which is an oddity of that game. Being such a blunt speaker, Jack was more naturally adept at defensive leadership activities like tackling, heading, blocking, and bollocking.

Jack asked Bobby after the last horn: Well, what about that kinda? How about that?

Bobby then said to Jack, Jackie, our lives are never going to be the same.

Years later, Jack declined to say that 1966 was the pinnacle of his career because he felt like a latecomer in a group that included Ramsey's favorites, such as Bobby. Instead, the more senior Charlton chose Leeds United's championship triumph in 1969.

The Holy Trinity of Best, Law, and Charlton, the yardstick by which all of Manchester United's front lines are assessed, included Bobby by that point. He had also won the European Cup and the World Cup. Bobby was quite high up. Although some of their performance was thrilling as well, Jack was a terrifying pillar of Revie's outlaw spirit at Leeds.

They became a powerful team on the field since their opposing playing styles complemented one another so well. Off the field, however, their dissimilar personalities frequently clashed.

The Charlton brothers' friendship was unshakable despite their differences. They had a strong sense of respect and regard for one another, and they were fiercely loyal to one another.

However, when their lives diverged, the chasm between them grew wider. Jack's calm and unpretentious life stood in stark contrast to Bobby's famous status and jet-set lifestyle.

Their relationship deteriorated subsequently due to conflicts and miscommunications brought on by their contrasting worldviews.

But despite their growing separation, they still shared a brotherly closeness.

Conflict between Cissie Charlton and Norma, Bobby's wife, led to the dissolution of their relationship. Jack discussed the schism on Desert Island Discs in 1996, saying, I couldn't understand why there was a rift between Bobby and my mother. He abruptly decided not to go home. I'm not sure why. Sue Lawley questioned Jack about whether the harm was irreparable, and Jack responded, I think so.

Bobby finally spoke up in his memoirs published in 2007: My wife has a very strong temperament and does not put up with fools gladly. I don't want to imply that my mother was a fool. There was a clash, and it essentially never subsided.

Jack made comments about my wife that were completely despicable when he appeared in the tabloids. Nonsense. 'Hoity-toity' is not a word my wife would use; just ask anyone who has ever met her. My brother erred greatly. I fail to comprehend why he did it. He was unable to have both known her and said what he did.

For Ray Wilson's funeral in 2018, the dispute was set aside. But there was still a rift between the two. On a honeyed day in 1966, their lives followed parallel paths that came together gloriously before splitting off once more, as if to show everyone how flimsy and contingent sibling ties can be. They are now on par with death due to the pandemic of dementia.

Jack Charlton has a place in the paradise of football. He now comes into the world in his unique light as our kid, as he dubbed his younger sibling. Bobby Charlton would be the name that, if it had to be used to describe the spirit of English football, would be recited.

Two brothers who reached fame together but whose dissimilar personalities caused them to take different routes in life are the subjects of Bobby and Jack Charlton's narrative.

It serves as a reminder that the demands of achievement and the pressures of fame can put even the closest of relationships to the test.

The Charlton brothers are two of the greatest football players of all time, and despite their differences, their legacy will continue to motivate future generations.

Chapter seven

The Charitable Contributions and Humanitarian Side of Sir Bobby Charlton's Life: The Sir Bobby Charlton Foundation

Football star Sir Bobby Charlton established the Sir Bobby Charlton Foundation in 2011, which is a charity with UK charitable registration.

Sir Bobby saw firsthand the devastation that landmines and the legacy of a long-forgotten conflict were still inflicting on innocent civilian communities while touring a minefield in Cambodia. After visiting Cambodia, Sir Bobby Charlton was inspired to found the charity so that he could take concrete action to assist the individuals he had seen there and countless more like them throughout the world.

When the organization first began, its efforts to alleviate the effects of the war were concentrated on creating new technology for better detecting landmines and explosive relics of war and on enhancing surgical methods for those who had sustained limb loss and explosive blast injuries. The foundation has evolved to provide more direct assistance to communities affected by war as a result of the groundbreaking work that is still being done today.

Sir Bobby was knighted in 1997 and is well-known throughout the world for his skill on the football field and his role as a selfless ambassador for the game. He is less well-known for his outstanding charitable work, particularly the creation of the Sir Bobby Charlton Foundation more than ten years ago, a non-profit organization devoted to aiding victims of warfare in conflict zones all over the world.

Through his kindness, concern, and unwaveringly strong ideals, Sir Bobby supported beneficiaries both domestically and abroad throughout his life as a tireless advocate for society's most vulnerable members.

Through his work with the Foundation, Sir Bobby was able to support both the longer-term development needs of individuals still dealing with the effects of earlier wars as well as the suffering of those caught up in current hostilities.

Outside of the stadiums and floodlights, Sir Bobby was dedicated to using his worldwide renown to raise awareness of the suffering of the underprivileged and give voice to the voiceless.

The Sir Bobby Charlton Foundation devotes the majority of its funding to aiding civilian populations in underdeveloped nations where ongoing and former hostilities exacerbate discrimination, poverty, and disadvantage. The charity's work, which supports the United Nations' 2030 Agenda for Sustainable Development, strives to use its strategy to make communities safer and more sustainable and to give locals the power to regain control over their lives and determine the course of their destinies.

Support provided by the Sir Bobby Charlton Foundation to areas affected by armed conflict takes many different forms, but each one aims to lessen suffering, abolish discrimination, and help recipients reach their full potential.

To assist those who have escaped the crisis in Syria, Iraq, and Yemen, The Sir Bobby Charlton Foundation conflict recovery center was established in 2017 in Amman, Jordan.

The facility features a physical therapy area, individual and group counseling rooms, and training classes, and it is accessible to those with disabilities. The assistance provided includes guidance with advanced prosthetic and orthotic care, child trauma, peer support, physical therapy, and other mobility aids.

Chapter eight

Global Recognition: Honors, Praise, and Awards

In 1966, Charlton assisted England in winning its lone FIFA World Cup victory, making it one of his most enduring accomplishments. He was essential to the team's success and scored twice against Portugal in the semifinal.

Between 1956 and 1973, Sir Bobby Charlton made 758 appearances for Manchester United. He rose to become the club's all-time leading scorer during this time, a title he kept up until 2017.

Sir Bobby Charlton received the Ballon d'Or in 1966 as a result of his outstanding performances.

The world's top football player receives this honor each year.

In the catastrophic Munich air crash of 1958, which also took the lives of eight of his Manchester United colleagues, Charlton was one of the survivors. His perseverance and resolve are demonstrated by his recuperation and subsequent return to football.

With 49 goals for the England national team, Charlton held the record for most goals scored for that team for almost 50 years. Till 2015, this record was the best.

Sir Bobby Charlton received the English Footballer of the Year award in 1974. He also won the BBC Sports Personality of the Year Lifetime Achievement Award in 2008.

A stand was named after him by Manchester United in 2016 to honor his enormous contribution to the team. Old Trafford's Sir Bobby Charlton Stand is evidence of his legendary fame.

After his playing career ended, Charlton transitioned into management. He was most notable as the manager of Preston North End and the interim manager of Wigan Athletic.

In addition to his achievements on the field, Charlton has promoted the game. He was crucial to England's success in its 2006 and 2018 World Cup bids.

Bobby Charlton was knighted by Queen Elizabeth II in 1994 in appreciation of his contributions to football, making him Sir Bobby Charlton.

He scored on his England debut, but the 4-0 loss to Scotland in 1958 overshadowed the achievement.

During a friendly match for Manchester United versus the Los Angeles Wolves in 1960 while on a U.S. tour, Charlton scored three goals in less than 10 minutes.

A testimonial game honoring Charlton's 17-year United career was staged in 1972 between Manchester United and a team made up of players from Celtic and Scotland.

Sir Bobby Charlton also received the esteemed Oxonian award from the illustrious Oxford Guild of the University of Oxford.

Trustees and officials of the Sir Bobby Charlton Foundation and the Oxford Guild attended the award ceremony, which was held on November 18, 2022, at the National Football Museum. Sir Bobby received the award in recognition of his accomplishments as a national and international athletic legend and to honor his remarkable service to charity and sport, including his role in helping England win the 1966 World Cup.

The University of Oxford bestows the honor in recognition of recipients' exceptional contributions to their field and beyond. The honor also recognized the best individuals who have made outstanding contributions to society and personified the principles upheld by Oxford Guild members.

The Oxford Guild, one of the oldest and biggest student organizations at the University of Oxford, is also one of the biggest in the entire world.

Despite being a more recent honor, The Oxonian has already been given to several deserving individuals, including Her Late Majesty Queen Elizabeth II and Former US President Jimmy Carter.

Sir Bobby Charlton Foundation chairman and esteemed trustee Stephen Cross graciously accepted the honor on Sir Bobby's behalf. Brahma Mohanty, managing director of The Oxford Guild, presented the prize.

Sir Bobby remains one of the select few England players with the most caps and goals scored in history. He rounded off a remarkable 1966 by winning the Ballon d'Or, establishing himself as one of the greatest footballers in history.

The foundation bearing Sir Bobby's name, which is devoted to promoting global development and championing the human rights we take for granted but for which some people still fight, truly embodies his love and passion for people, communities, and society, which extend far beyond the borders of these British Isles. The relentless efforts of people connected to the foundation ensure that Sir Bobby's commitment and beliefs continue to serve as a voice for those who cannot be heard and a catalyst for global social change.

Chapter nine

Fan Homages and Tributes: Messages from Fans

During the English Premier League match in the ninth week, sad news broke among the shouts of the crowd. Sir Bobby Charlton, a great of Manchester United and the England national team, passed away on Saturday evening (October 21, 2023, WIB).

His family, along with MU, directly broke the news. Before kickoff, the moment of silence—originally intended to honor the Israeli-Hamas war dead—was extended in honor of Charlton.

We regret to inform you that Sir Bobby passed away peacefully on Saturday morning. His relatives surrounded him. The family would like to convey their appreciation to everyone who helped with his care, as well as the numerous individuals who support and adore him. The official statement from Bobby's family states, We ask that the family's privacy be respected at this time.

At their Premier League encounter against Sheffield United on Saturday, October 21, Manchester United players wore black armbands, and a planned minute of silence was extended to honor Charlton. Fans started to place flower tributes at Old Trafford in the meantime.

A book of condolences will be available to fans and the general public on Sunday at 10 a.m., the club announced. The club stated in a statement that Sir Bobby will always be remembered as a giant of the game.

Gareth Southgate, the manager of England, added his tribute, saying, I had the luxury of meeting him several times, which allowed me to grasp his pride and emotion in having served England, and it simply underlined in my mind his reputation as one of the gentlemen of the game.

The football community will come together in mourning the loss of an undisputed legend.

His accomplishments with the national team carried over to the club level as well. Charlton spent the majority of his career with Manchester United. After helping MU win their first European Cup in the club's history in 1968,

Charlton also rose to fame there. The final game was against Benfica, and Charlton scored twice.

Millions of people throughout the world view Sir Bobby as a hero, not just in Manchester or England but in every country where football is played. In addition to his outstanding skill as a football player, he is recognized for his sportsmanship and ethics. Sir Bobby will always be regarded as a football great, Manchester United declared in a statement posted on its official website.

Sir Geoff Hurst, a former teammate of Charlton's and the lone survivor of England's 1966 World Cup-winning squad, gave the icon his emotional tribute.

Very sad news today. One of the true greats, Sir Bobby Charlton, has passed away, the 81-year-old retired striker posted. He, as well as all of football, will never be forgotten by us.

More than just the sports community, the entire nation will miss him dearly. He was a fantastic friend and colleague. Geoff and Judith offer their condolences to his family and friends.

Sir Bobby Charlton, who passed away at the age of 86, was praised as a true great by Prince William.

Among those honoring one of the nation's greatest football players of all time is the 41-year-old Prince of Wales, president of the Football Association (FA).

Sir Bobby Charlton, the royal, wrote on X. Winner of the first division. Champion in Europe. Global champion. Legendary gentleman.

A real legend who will live on forever I'm grateful, Sir Bobby.

Sir Bobby Charlton passed away at the age of 86, and George Best's sister and her husband claim that they have lost a friend as a result.

Barbara McNarry, nee Best's husband, Norman McNarry, has spoken of the couple's grief at the legendary Manchester United and England player's loss.

All I can say is that Sir Bobby Charlton has been lost as a friend to Barbara and me.

He was a dependable friend who stood by us in good times and bad.

Sir Bobby's passing, according to Norman, is shocking but not unexpected.

Bobby wasn't present when we were at Old Trafford a few weeks ago to mark the 60th anniversary of George's debut match for Manchester United; we believed this was due to his health.

Norman refuted claims that George and Bobby were involved in a fight that started in the 1970s.

In an interview with the press in 1988, a reporter questioned George about the conflict and noted that Bobby had only expressed nice things about his former teammate.

If you watch any old film clips and shots of the game, I think you know, if he scored, I was the first there to congratulate him and voice praise, he stated.

Because we were teammates who had a common goal while we played.

But off the pitch, he lived his life, and I lived mine. He was a devoted father.

He went home to the family, and I went out, and you know.

The notion that the two weren't friends was debunked, according to Norman.

When George was ill, Bobby expressly came to the hospital to see him, the man recalled.

To me, that seems like a friend-like action.

Numerous sports figures, including Denis Law, former Manchester United manager Sir Alex Ferguson, and former England manager Sven-Goran Eriksson, attended George's burial at Stormont on December 3, 2005. Sir Bobby Charlton was one of them.

The Irish FA has paid tribute to the important part of the England team that won the 1966 World Cup, which also included Jack Charlton, his younger brother, who later managed the Republic of Ireland and led the side to the World Cup in 1990 and 1994.

With United, who made history by becoming the first English team to win the European Cup in 1968, Sir Bobby Charlton also achieved enormous success at the club level.

The Irish FA tweeted on X, The news of Sir Bobby Charlton's passing is deeply saddening to everyone at the Irish FA.

His friends and family, as well as everyone associated with Manchester United and England, are in our thoughts and prayers.

His accomplishments are so enormous that he is now a legend and a giant who has died. What he accomplished is amazing on a global scale, not just in England, said Red Devils manager Erik ten Hag following his team's Premier League victory at Sheffield United on Saturday night.

All the games, all the titles, all the trophies, all the goals he scored

I never had the privilege of meeting him, but I heard that despite all of his victories and awards, he was quite modest. a strong character and role model for all of us, both as a football player and in global culture. I've heard that several players found inspiration in it and yearned for victory to celebrate it. It served as an additional impetus.

Before kickoff at Bramall Lane, club captain Bruno Fernandes laid a wreath in remembrance of Charlton, and both sets of players and supporters participated in a minute of applause.

Former and current Manchester United players were eager to express their appreciation for Charlton after learning that he had survived the devastating Munich flight accident in 1958, which claimed the lives of 23 individuals, including eight of his United teammates.

David Beckham, who made his Manchester United debut at the age of 17 and later attended Charlton's soccer academy, claimed that Sir Bobby was the reason I had the opportunity to play for Manchester United. I owe everything to Sir Bobby.

Rooney, the all-time leading scorer for Manchester United, claimed he was still in disbelief after managing Birmingham City for the first time on Saturday against Middlesbrough. We learned the news as we exited the stadium for the second half at halftime.

He's had a terrific life, it was said, winning the World Cup in '66 and the European Cup in '68 after all he'd been through with the Munich disaster. He is a fantastic player and a true legend.

He is a well-known character all around the world, said Middlesbrough manager Michael Carrick, who played for Old Trafford for 12 years.

I had the good fortune to get to know him, experience his support, and see how much he valued Manchester United. I never took that status for granted.

On X (previously Twitter), former Manchester United goalkeeper Alex Stepney posted: A big loss for the game. A magnificent player and man. So many wonderful moments were had. Bless you, Bobby; it was an honor.

The Red Devils paid their heartfelt homage, referring to Charlton as one of the greatest and most beloved players in our club's history.

Sir Bobby was a hero to millions, not just in Manchester or the United Kingdom, but wherever football is played around the world, they stated.

Sir Bobby will always be regarded as a giant of the game because of his tremendous athletic abilities as well as his sportsmanship and honesty.

Manager of Manchester City, Pep Guardiola: A tremendous loss for his family, the family of Manchester United, and for English and European football.

a famous figure. We offer our sympathies to his family, Manchester United, and everyone else on behalf of Manchester City because it is because of people like these that the Premier League exists.

Former Manchester United and England defender Rio Ferdinand: Sir Bobby, legend, greatness, icon When compared to a man of Sir Bobby's caliber, these remarks are made by all of us to numerous people who completely lack merit.

One of the original Busby Babes, according to former Manchester United defender Gary Neville. At Manchester United, he won youth championships. Later, he won the European Cup and the World Cup. In the contemporary period, he served as the club's director. He was without a doubt the finest player and representative of English football. A winner both on and off the field.

Former Arsenal defender Martin Keown: He was an enormous talent and a very outstanding player. He has recently been a fantastic representative for Manchester United. He was such a classy man and will go on in memory for a very long time because of the way he handled himself.

Chapter ten

Personal Life: Love, Loss, and Willpower

The world honors Bobby's contributions to football, but Norma Ball, Bobby Charlton's wife, was also a remarkable person.

Bobby had Norma Ball by his side during the highs and lows of his illustrious career, supporting him through difficult times like the Munich Air Disaster in 1958 but also celebrating triumphs like the 1966 World Cup victory. In 2020, she showed remarkable bravery by publicly disclosing that Bobby had been battling dementia in the hopes that their story might help others dealing with the same difficulties.

The renowned footballer Sir Bobby Charlton leaves behind a loving family that includes his longtime partner, Norma Ball, as well as a history of outstanding accomplishments on the field.

Norma, who was very reticent about her personal life, first met Bobby in Manchester in 1959 at an ice rink. after spending two years courting before deciding to be married.

Bobby is a true footballer who has never been in trouble or been in a fight with the officials, and even less so with opponents. He is also a loving husband who has nothing but affection for the subdued Norma (née Ball). Norma became Bobby's ally once he married her in 1991, and vice versa. She established herself as a mainstay in the infamous WAGs group of well-known players. However, she and Bobby continued to live modestly, which was unusual even among legendary football players in the 1960s and 1970s.

Two daughters, Suzanne and Andrea, were born to Sir Bobby Charlton and Norma Ball. In the 1960s, Suzanne worked as a weather forecaster for the BBC and made a lot of contributions on her own.

Robert, Suzanne's son, is named after his well-known grandfather.

Despite his fame as a footballing golden kid and a global superstar, Bobby, and Norma, née Ball, were both by nature quiet people.

But everyone who knew them could see how strong their loving relationship was; it even contributed to a family fight.

On July 30, 1966, Norma was present at Wembley Stadium to witness Bobby and his teammates' World Cup victory.

Days earlier, against Portugal, he scored two unstoppable goals that guaranteed the Three Lions' spot in the championship game when they defeated West Germany 4-2.

She also went to Buckingham Palace with him when he was knighted in July 1994.

The long-standing conflict between Sir Bobby and his older brother Jack, who also played on that World Cup-winning team, was rarely discussed.

However, he did discuss it in 2007, stating that, in addition to Jack, there was conflict between his wife and his mother, Cissie.

And he disclosed that, given an option, he supported his wife.

Norma Ball stands out in the world of celebrity weddings for her resolve to live a secret existence free from prying eyes. She is not known to have any official social media accounts, and little is known about her current activities. Therefore, it is imperative to respect the family's right to privacy as they process the death of a dear family member.

Sir Bobby Charlton and Norma Ball Charlton's entwined lives are a monument to love, devotion, and a common goal. Their combined legacy—which includes accomplishments on the football field and noteworthy charitable work—remains a light for many.

Chapter eleven

The Best Bobby Charlton Sayings

Some claim that we professional soccer players are slaves to the game. Give me a life sentence if this is enslavement.

Football is the only game that requires invention due to the breadth of its appeal and its capacity to touch every aspect of humanity.

The only person to whom I truly felt inferior, even now, was Duncan Edwards. I've never met anybody with the combination of talent, strength, and presence that he possessed.

I'm not hesitant to identify the person who embodies all that football to me by name. This is

Paul Scholes. people like George Best and Denis Law, who I cherished having as teammates, and now, people I have closely followed during the Alex Ferguson period. And Scholes is my favorite in so many ways. I admire his wit and certainty that he will make the pivotal pass or deliver the winning volley.

Even though it was questionable whether the punishment was within or outside the box, it was a reasonable decision.

I love Paul Scholes as a player. He personifies both the Manchester United spirit and all that is admirable about football.

Messi has likely accomplished more currently than most players, in my opinion. However, he is in the same league as Pelé, Johan Cruyff, and

Alfredo de Stefano. He will automatically become one of them when he completes his work and retires. While the game of football is as wonderful and popular as it is, there will always be a player that people talk about. He is a terrific player.

Beckham is distinctive. He yearned hard to play football. When he was nine or ten, his mind was set. Many young people believe they cannot do it. But to succeed in any sport, you must practice.

Wayne Rooney has the potential to be one of the biggest discoveries in international football, which is why I'm looking forward to the International Cup.

I'm quite impressed with Tottenham. Even though they have been under pressure, they haven't given up.

I'm not hesitant to identify the person who embodies all that football to me by name. This is Paul Scholes. My favorite author is Scholes in so many ways.

I enjoy watching young Paul Scholes because he seems to have complete control over his actions and constantly passes the ball with such accuracy and precision.

Chapter twelve

Net worth

Bobby Charlton's net worth rose to a respectable $40 million by 2023, which is about similar to £33 million. This enormous wealth is the consequence of his success in business, real estate, and wise investments, rather than just his time spent playing football.

In the 1960s, young Bobby had a $10,000 net worth. But thanks to his commitment to his art and the rising popularity of football, by 1980, he had $15 million in wealth. This amount increased to $19 million around the turn of the millennium, and by 2010, Sir Bobby's net worth was reported to be $31 million.

Fewer people are aware of Sir Bobby's successes off the field compared to his on-field accomplishments. Sir Bobby has proven to have an excellent sense of real estate. His extensive portfolio includes an outstanding range of properties, including both residential and commercial real estate, all around England.

The most valuable asset in Charlton's estate is his Northumberland home, which is worth more than £10 million. This property is more than just a house; it's a vast estate with an opulent country house, several cottages, and hundreds of acres of farmland. Additionally, Sir Bobby has homes in several important English cities, including a flat in the vibrant capital of London, a charming house in Manchester, and a vacation home in the lovely county of Cornwall.

Charlton has further business knowledge as well. He also dabbled in commercial real estate, acquiring the Trafford Centre, a well-known shopping center in Manchester, as well as several other office and retail structures.

The money Sir Bobby Charlton intends to leave behind will ensure that his legacy endures in addition to the achievements he made in football. His will dedicates a substantial 50% of his assets to his grandchildren, ensuring that they get the rewards of his life's labor.

Sir Bobby's path from a modest beginning to a net worth of $40 million is a monument to what is possible with a combination of talent, effort, and intelligence. The legacy of Sir Bobby Charlton will go on for many years thanks to his success in sports and his enormous riches.

Chapter thirteen

Conclusion

The life of Sir Bobby Charlton is a motivational example of talent, commitment, and wise decisions.

The legendary accomplishments, moral integrity, and dedication of Sir Bobby Charlton will live on in the annals of Manchester United and English football. The life-changing work of the Sir Bobby Charlton Foundation will continue his legacy.

The passing of Sir Bobby Charlton signifies the end of an era in football. He had an immeasurable influence on both the game and the lives of those he touched. We honor this football legend's incredible career, his unfailing sportsmanship, and his commitment to the noble game as we remember him.

Sir Bobby Charlton, one of the greatest players to ever take the field, will go down in football history for all time.

A week after his 86th birthday, he passed away, leaving an enduring hole in the football community.

In a nutshell, football fans continue to remember and honor the Charlton brothers' lives and careers, which were entwined with harmony and discord.

Rip.

Printed in Great Britain
by Amazon

34749017R00062